Taking Off

Literacy Workbook

Christy M. Newman

McGraw-Hill
ESL/ELT

Taking Off Literacy Workbook, 1st Edition

Published by McGraw-Hill ESL/ELT, a business unit of The McGraw-Hill Companies, Inc., 1221 Avenue of the Americas, New York, NY 10020. Copyright © 2004 by The McGraw-Hill Companies, Inc. All rights reserved. No part of this publication may be reproduced or distributed in any form or by any means, or stored in a database or retrieval system, without the prior written consent of The McGraw-Hill Companies, Inc., including, but not limited to, in any network or other electronic storage or transmission, or broadcast for distance learning.

This book is printed on recycled, acid-free paper containing 10% postconsumer waste.

1 2 3 4 5 6 7 8 9 0 QPD 0 9 8 7 6 5 4 3 2 1

ISBN 0-07-285950-4
Editorial director: Tina B. Carver
Senior managing editor: Erik Gundersen
Developmental editors: Linda O'Roke, Mari Vargo
Director of North American marketing: Thomas P. Dare
Production manager: Juanita Thompson
Interior designer: Eileen Wagner
Art: Mick Reid

The *Taking Off* Literacy Workbook has been designed for literacy students enrolled in low beginning classes. Most low beginning students are true beginners in English who are literate in their first language. Literacy students, on the other hand, usually do not have fundamental first-language literacy skills. Literacy students often need specific instruction in letter formation and other fundamental reading, listening, and writing skills.

As teachers who have worked with mixed groups of literacy and low beginning students know, dealing simultaneously with the needs of each of these groups of learners is a great challenge. The Literacy Workbook offers a unique resource for teachers in such multi-level classes. Each Literacy Workbook unit provides essential support for key elements of the *Taking Off* Student Book. Working with or without a teacher's aide, literacy students can tackle basic reading, listening, and writing activities in the Literacy Workbook while students with literacy skills in their first language can take on the tasks in the Workbook.

The *Taking Off* Literacy Workbook is divided into two sections. Section 1 contains 37 pages of basic literacy and numeracy exercises. These exercises focus on identifying and writing both upper case and lower case letters and the numbers 0-10. Section 2 contains four pages of literacy support for each unit in the Student Book. Eight Writing practice pages appear at the end of the Workbook for students who need additional practice with forming letters

A special audiocassette/CD for the Literacy Workbook offers additional listening practice for literacy students.

Table of Contents

Table of Contents

Table of Contents

Section 1 Letter and number practice

TILH

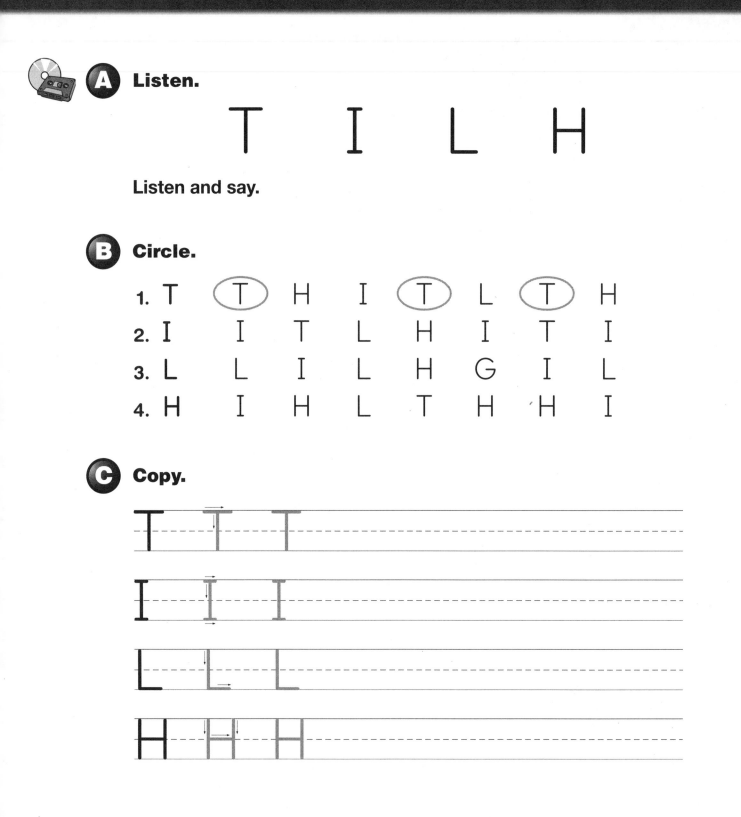

A Listen.

T I L H

Listen and say.

B Circle.

1. T (T) H I (T) L (T) H
2. I I T L H I T I
3. L L I L H G I L
4. H I H L T H H I

C Copy.

T | T T

I | I I

L | L L

H | H H

A **Listen.**

E F A Y X

Listen and say.

B **Circle.**

1. E (E) H F (E) T L (E)
2. F I F E H F F E
3. A Y A Y A X A H
4. Y Y X A H Y Z Y
5. X A X H X Y X H

C **Copy.**

E E E

F F F

A A A

Y Y Y

X X X

A Listen.

N M V W K

Listen and say.

B Circle.

1. N   (N)   M   X   (N)   (N)   W   Y
2. M   W   M   V   M   X   M   A
3. V   W   A   V   V   N   M   V
4. W   W   M   N   V   W   W   M
5. K   H   K   K   M   X   Y   K

C Copy.

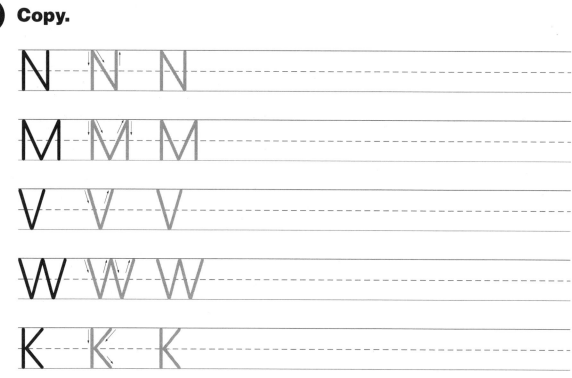

Listening practice 1

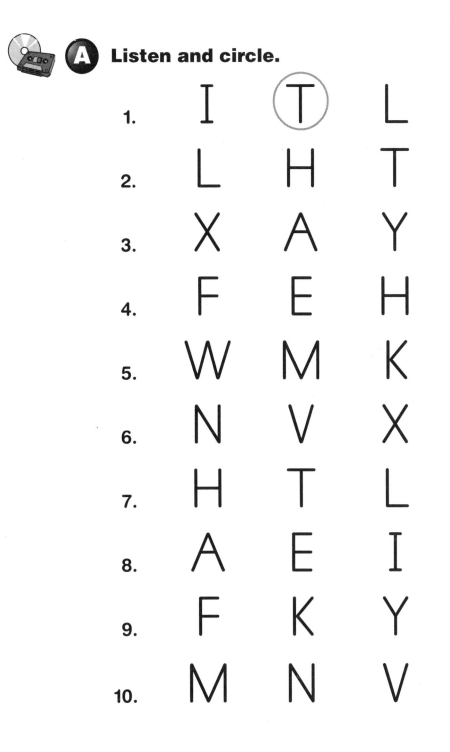

A Listen and circle.

1.	I	(T)	L
2.	L	H	T
3.	X	A	Y
4.	F	E	H
5.	W	M	K
6.	N	V	X
7.	H	T	L
8.	A	E	I
9.	F	K	Y
10.	M	N	V

U C O Q

 **A** **Listen.**

U   C   O   Q

Listen and say.

B **Circle.**

1. U   C   O   Ⓤ   V   C   Ⓤ Ⓤ
2. C   C   O   Q   C   U   D   C
3. O   U   O   C   O   O   D   Q
4. Q   O   Q   D   Q   D   O   Q

C **Copy.**

U U U

C C C

O O O

Q Q Q

P R B D

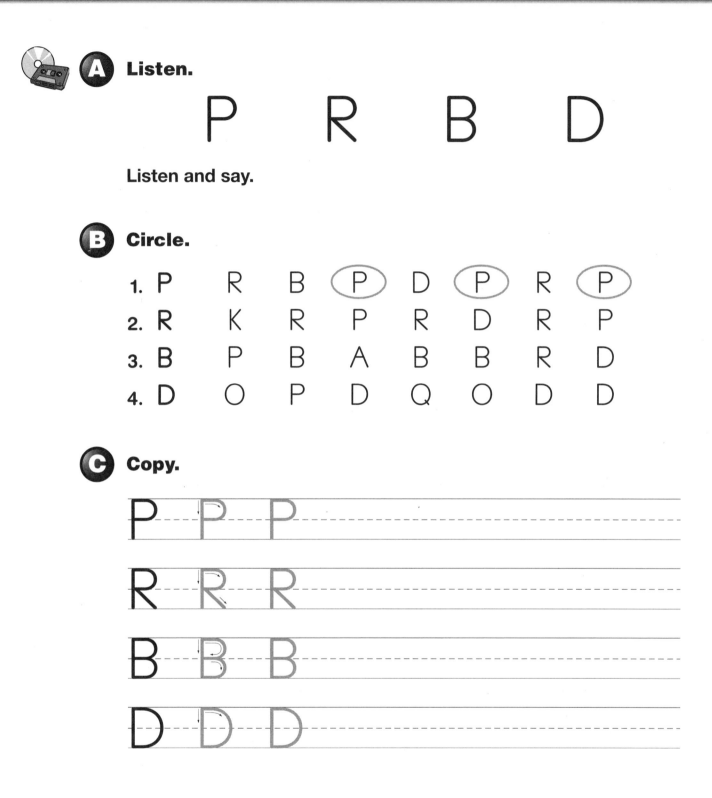

A Listen.

P R B D

Listen and say.

B Circle.

1. P   R   B   (P)   D   (P)   R   (P)
2. R   K   R   P   R   D   R   P
3. B   P   B   A   B   B   R   D
4. D   O   P   D   Q   O   D   D

C Copy.

P — P — P

R — R — R

B — B — B

D — D — D

S G J Z

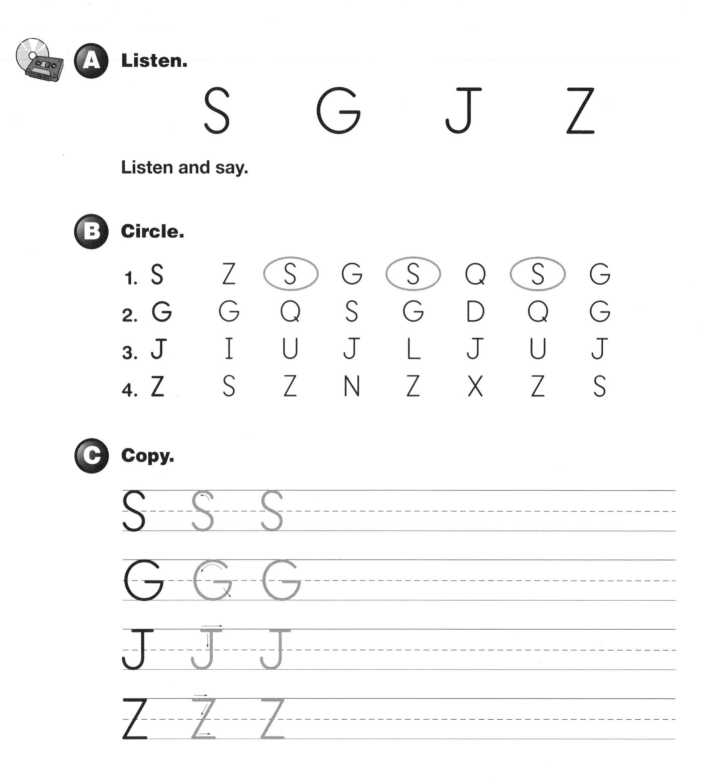

A Listen.

S   G   J   Z

Listen and say.

B Circle.

1. S   Z   (S)   G   (S)   Q   (S)   G
2. G   G   Q   S   G   D   Q   G
3. J   I   U   J   L   J   U   J
4. Z   S   Z   N   Z   X   Z   S

C Copy.

S   S   S

G   G   G

J   J   J

Z   Z   Z

Listening practice 2

A Listen and circle.

1.   U   O   (Q)

2.   C   Q   U

3.   P   B   D

4.   R   D   T

5.   J   G   S

6.   G   S   Z

7.   O   D   G

8.   S   C   R

9.   Z   J   P

10.   G   B   U

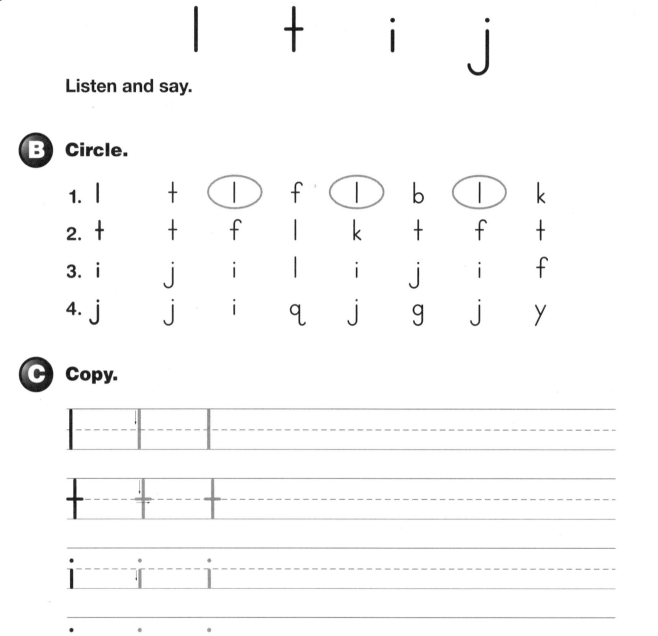

A **Listen.**

l   t   i   j

Listen and say.

B **Circle.**

1. l   t   (l)   f   (l)   b   (l)   k
2. t   t   f   l   k   t   f   t
3. i   j   i   l   i   j   i   f
4. j   j   i   q   j   g   j   y

C **Copy.**

V W X Z

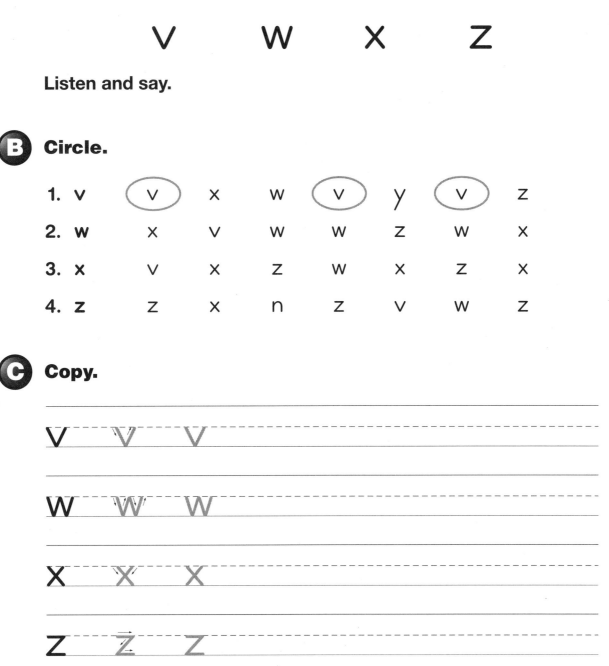

A **Listen.**

V   W   X   Z

Listen and say.

B **Circle.**

1. v   (v)   x   w   (v)   y   (v)   z

2. w   x   v   w   w   z   w   x

3. x   v   x   z   w   x   z   x

4. z   z   x   n   z   v   w   z

C **Copy.**

V V V

W W W

X X X

Z Z Z

A Listen.

o   c   a   e   s

Listen and say.

B Circle.

1. **o**   a   ⟨o⟩   c   ⟨o⟩   ⟨o⟩   e   a
2. **c**   e   c   a   o   c   c   e
3. **a**   a   d   e   a   o   c   a
4. **e**   e   c   e   a   o   e   c
5. **s**   c   s   e   s   s   a   c

C Copy.

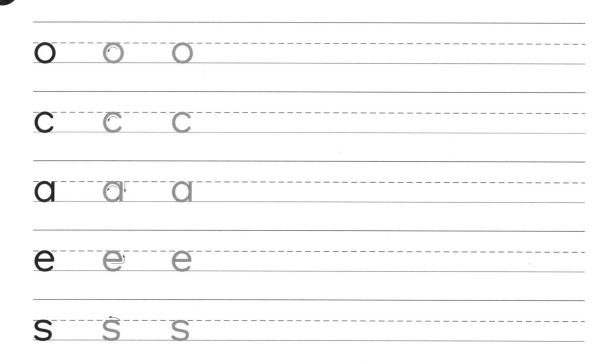

O   O   O

C   C   C

a   a   a

e   e   e

s   s   s

Listening practice 3

A Listen and circle.

1. l ⟨t⟩ j

2. i l t

3. s w z

4. v m w

5. s e a

6. c o e

7. v c t

8. e o a

9. x j c

10. l z t

A Listen.

u   r   n   h   m

Listen and say.

B Circle.

1. u   m   (u)   n   o   (u)   (u)   r
2. r   r   n   u   m   u   r   r
3. n   m   u   n   n   h   u   n
4. h   h   n   u   h   w   h   p
5. m   n   m   b   d   m   h   m

C Copy.

u   u   u

r   r   r

n   n   n

h   h   h

m   m   m

b d p q

A Listen.

b d p q

Listen and say.

B Circle.

1. b   d   h   (b) (b)   p   (b)   d
2. d   b   d   a   d   b   b   d
3. p   g   p   p   q   y   p   j
4. q   g   q   p   q   p   q   y

C Copy.

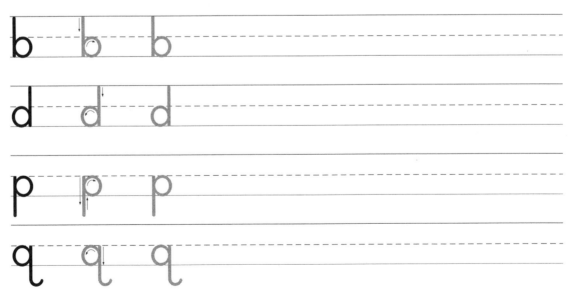

Section One

A **Listen.**

y g f k

Listen and say.

B **Circle.**

1. y   g   ⓨ   ⓨ   j   q   ⓨ   v
2. g   g   q   g   g   q   j   y
3. f   f   f   t   t   h   f   k
4. k   k   h   x   k   l   f   k

C **Copy.**

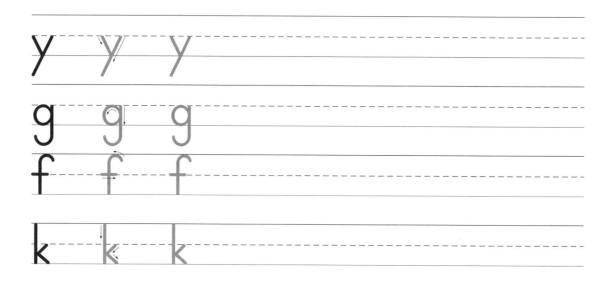

A **Listen and circle.**

1. g (u) r

2. h m k

3. p d q

4. h b d

5. k l f

6. g j y

7. h f b

8. y m n

9. p b g

10. r g q

Upper and lower case letter practice

 A **Listen.**

Aa Bb Cc Dd

Listen and say.

 B **Listen and circle.**

1. B   C   (D)
2. D   A   C
3. c   b   a
4. b   a   d

C **Copy.**

Upper Case Letters	Lower Case Letters
1. A A A _____	a a a _____
2. B B B _____	b b b _____
3. C C C _____	c c c _____
4. D D D _____	d d d _____

Upper and lower case letter practice

A Listen.

E e F f G g H h

Listen and say.

B Listen and circle.

1. H (G) F
2. E F H
3. f e h
4. h f g

C Copy.

Upper Case Letters	Lower Case Letters

1. E E E _ _ _ _ _   e e e _ _ _ _ _
2. F F F _ _ _ _ _   f f f _ _ _ _ _
3. G G G _ _ _ _ _   g g g _ _ _ _ _
4. H H H _ _ _ _ _   h h h _ _ _ _ _

Upper and lower case letter practice

A **Listen.**

Ii   Jj   Kk   Ll

Listen and say.

B **Listen and circle.**

1. (J)   K   L

2. L   I   K

3. k   l   i

4. i   j   l

C **Copy.**

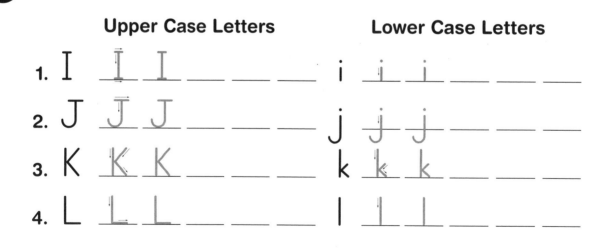

Upper Case Letters		Lower Case Letters	
1. I	I I ___ ___	i	i i ___ ___
2. J	J J ___ ___	j	j j ___ ___
3. K	K K ___ ___	k	k k ___ ___
4. L	L L ___ ___	l	l l ___ ___

Upper and lower case letter practice

 A **Listen.**

Mm Nn Oo Pp

Listen and say.

 B **Listen and circle.**

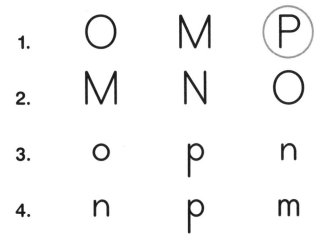

1. O M (P)

2. M N O

3. o p n

4. n p m

C **Copy.**

Upper Case Letters	Lower Case Letters
1. M M M _____	m m m _____
2. N N N _____	n n n _____
3. O O O _____	o o o _____
4. P P P _____	p p p _____

Upper and lower case letter practice

A Listen.

Qq Rr Ss Tt Uu

Listen and say.

B Listen and circle.

1. ⓇR   S   Q

2. T   R   U

3. r   u   q

4. t   r   s

C Copy.

Upper Case Letters	Lower Case Letters
1. Q Q Q _____	q q q _____
2. R R R _____	r r r _____
3. S S S _____	s s s _____
4. T T T _____	t t t _____
5. U U U _____	u u u _____

Upper and lower case letter practice

 A **Listen.**

Vv Ww Xx Yy Zz

Listen and say.

B **Listen and circle.**

1. (V) Y W
2. W X Z
3. y z x
4. w v y

C **Copy.**

Upper Case Letters	Lower Case Letters
1. V V V _ _ _	v v v _ _ _
2. W W W _ _ _	w w w _ _ _
3. X X X _ _ _	x x x _ _ _
4. Y Y Y _ _ _	y y y _ _ _
5. Z Z Z _ _ _	z z z _ _ _

Upper and lower case letter practice

A **Match.**

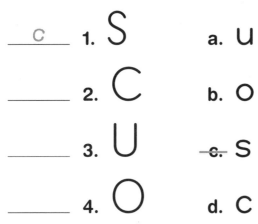

_c_	1. S	a.	u
___	2. C	b.	o
___	3. U	~~c.~~	s
___	4. O	d.	c

B **Match.**

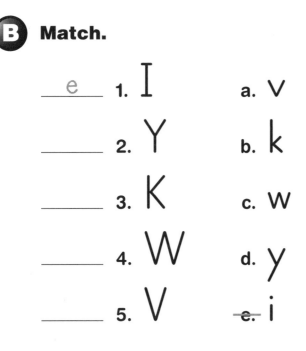

_e_	1. I	a.	v
___	2. Y	b.	k
___	3. K	c.	w
___	4. W	d.	y
___	5. V	~~e.~~	i

Upper and lower case letter practice

 Circle the lower case letter.

1. N   m   h   (n)
2. F   t   f   l
3. L   h   i   l
4. A   a   o   c

 Circle the lower case letter.

1. H   h   n   d
2. R   n   r   k
3. E   e   o   c
4. G   q   p   g

C   **Circle the lower case letter.**

1. D   h   d   b
2. T   t   l   i
3. Q   g   j   q
4. B   b   h   d
5. R   n   m   r

Upper case letters in words

 A **Circle the letter.**

1. A (A)ND   CH(A)IR   T(A)LL
2. B BLUE   BOY   NOTEBOOK
3. C CLASS   NICE   COPY
4. D DON   DOOR   BOARD

 B **Circle the letter.**

1. E EIGHT   PAPER   PEN
2. F FIVE   FIRST   FOUR
3. G GRACE   EIGHT   GO
4. H HI   PHONE   THREE

 C **Circle the letter.**

1. I IS   NICE   THIS
2. J JAPAN   JOB   JOHNSON
3. K TALK   TAKE   KITCHEN
4. L CLASS   LAST   CLOSE
5. M MY   MEET   NAME

Upper case letters in words

 A **Circle the letter.**

1. N (N)O (N)AME O(N)
2. O ONE POINT YOU
3. P PEN PARK OPEN
4. Q QUICK QUIT QUEEN

 B **Circle the letter.**

1. R RED MARIA YOUR
2. S STREET CARLOS DESK
3. T TWO WHAT TIEN
4. U USA BLUE PUT

C **Circle the letter.**

1. V VERY FIVE LIVE
2. W WALK WHAT WEEK
3. X SIX EXIT TAXI
4. Y YES YOUR SAY
5. Z ZERO SIZE ZIP CODE

Lower case letters in words

 A **Circle the letter.**

1. a   ⓐn d   Chinⓐ   tⓐll
2. b   blue   number   boy
3. c   copy   chair   nice
4. d   do   door   and

B **Circle the letter.**

1. e   e-mail   paper   pen
2. f   five   first   of
3. g   go   eight   walking
4. h   hello   phone   what

 C **Circle the letter.**

1. i   is   nice   hi
2. j   jacket   job   jump
3. k   kitchen   book   talk
4. l   last   class   lunch

Lower case letters in words

 Circle the letter.

1. m   (m)y   (m)eet   na(m)e
2. n   no   name   on
3. o   one   your   you
4. p   pen   copy   open
5. q   quick   quit   quarter

 Circle the letter.

1. r   red   room   your
2. s   stop   speak   desk
3. t   two   what   three
4. u   up   you   put

C **Circle the letter.**

1. v   seven   five   live
2. w   write   brown   week
3. x   taxi   six   Mexico
4. y   yes   your   say
5. z   zero   size   zip code

Numbers 0–5

 A Listen.

0 zero   1 one   2 two

3 three   4 four   5 five

Listen and say.

B Copy.

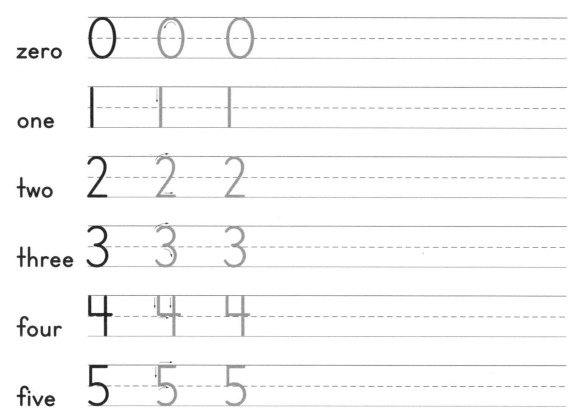

zero   0   0   0

one   1   1   1

two   2   2   2

three   3   3   3

four   4   4   4

five   5   5   5

Numbers 6–10

 A **Listen.**

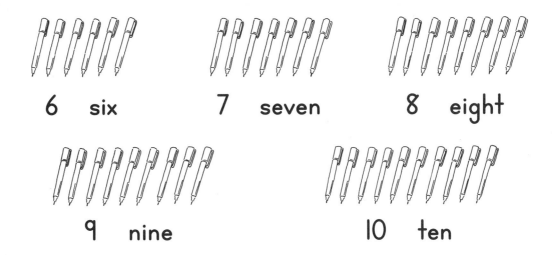

6 six   7 seven   8 eight

9 nine   10 ten

Listen and say.

B **Copy.**

six   6 6 6

seven   7 7 7

eight   8 8 8

nine   9 9 9

ten   10 10 10

Number practice

A **Circle.**

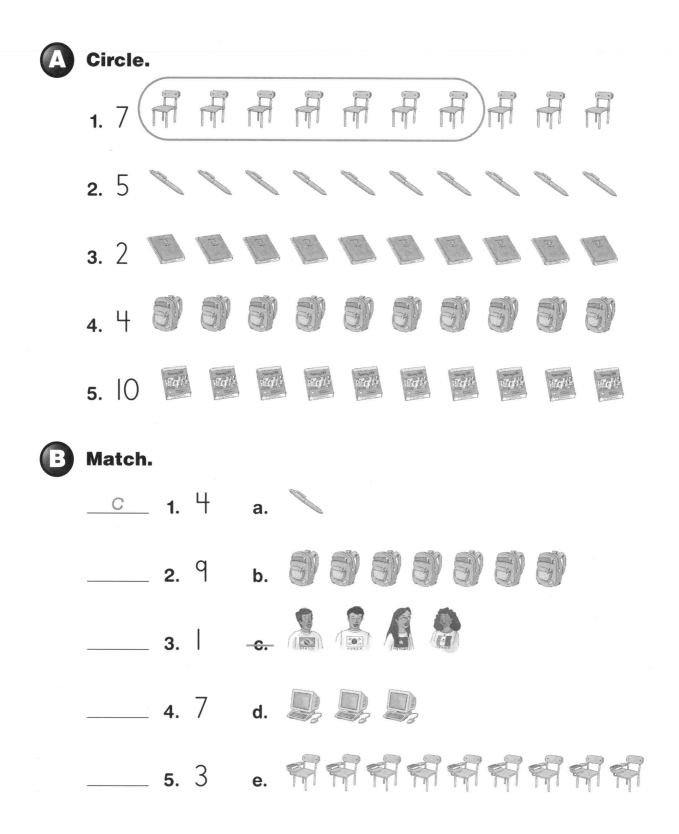

1. 7

2. 5

3. 2

4. 4

5. 10

B **Match.**

_c_ 1. 4   **a.**

___ 2. 9   **b.**

___ 3. 1   ~~c.~~

___ 4. 7   **d.**

___ 5. 3   **e.**

Number practice

A **Circle.**

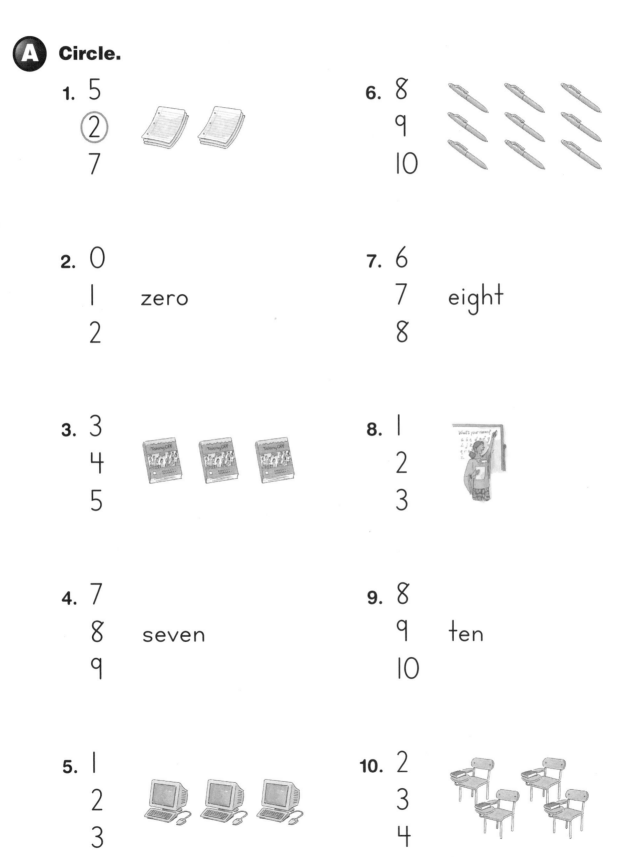

1. 5
   (2)
   7

2. 0
   1   zero
   2

3. 3
   4
   5

4. 7
   8   seven
   9

5. 1
   2
   3

6. 8
   9
   10

7. 6
   7   eight
   8

8. 1
   2
   3

9. 8
   9   ten
   10

10. 2
    3
    4

Number practice

A **Circle.**

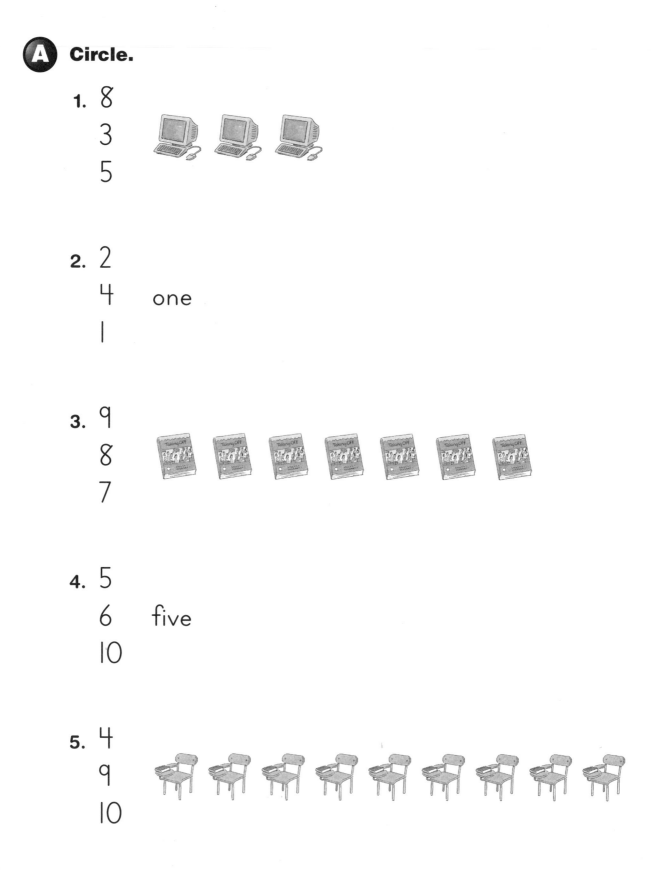

1. 8
   3
   5

2. 2
   4
   1   one

3. 9
   8
   7

4. 5
   6   five
   10

5. 4
   9
   10

Letter review

 A Listen.

ABCDEFGHIJKLM

Listen and say.

B Write.

A __ C D __ F __ H I J __ L __

 C Listen.

a b c d e f g h i j k l m

Listen and say.

D Write.

__ b c __ __ f g __ i __ k l m

 **E** Listen and circle.

1. G○   E   B   C

2. J   C   G   B

3. a   h   f   e

4. m   e   i   l

Letter review

 **A** Listen.

NOPQRSTUVWXYZ

Listen and say.

B Write.

N O __ Q __ __ T __ V __ X __ Z

 C Listen.

nopqrstuvwxyz

Listen and say.

D Write.

__ o __ __ __ s __ u v __ __ y __

 **E** Listen and circle.

1. X   K   S   (Z)

2. Q   O   C   G

3. w   s   z   y

4. u   v   m   w

Number review

A **Listen.**

0 1 2 3 4 5 6 7 8 9 10

Listen and say.

B **Write.**

__ 1 __ 3 4 __ __ 7 __ 9 __

C **Listen and circle.**

1.   5   0   1   4   2

2.   8   10   6   9   7

D **Copy.**

1	1	3 __	2 __
4 __	7 __	8 __
6 __	5 __	9 __

Section 2 Support exercises for Student Book

A Listen.

Ff   Ll   Nn

Listen and say.

B Write.

1. Ff   _F_ IRST   _f_ our
2. Ll   C __ OSE   __ isten
3. Nn   __ AME   __ ice

C Circle.

1. FIRST   (FIRST)   FIVE   FOUR
2. LAST   LIST   LEFT   LAST
3. name   nine   name   meet
4. notebook   book   computer   notebook

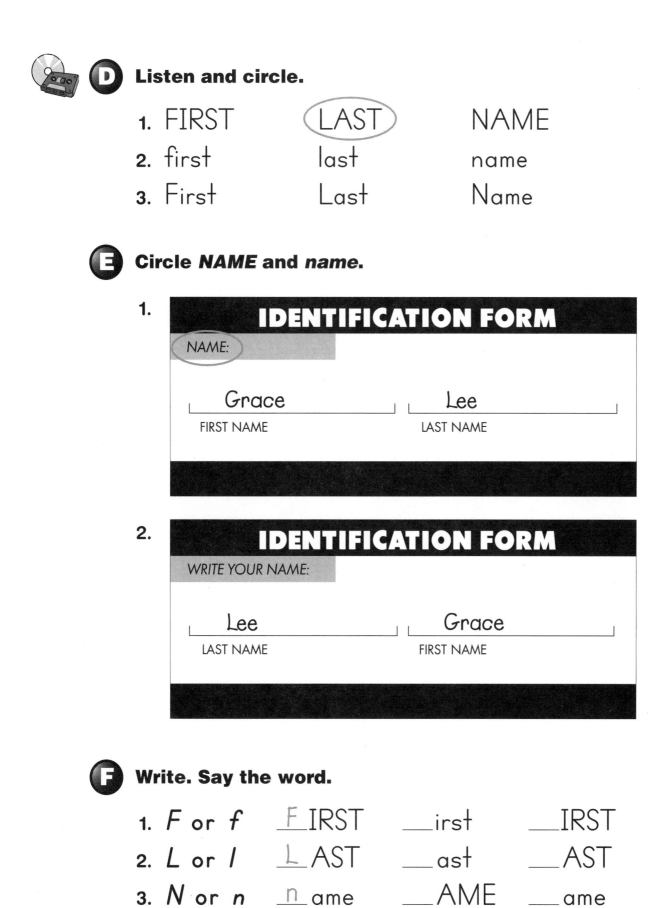

D Listen and circle.

1. FIRST   (LAST)   NAME
2. first   last   name
3. First   Last   Name

E Circle NAME and name.

1.

IDENTIFICATION FORM

(NAME:)

Grace   Lee
FIRST NAME   LAST NAME

2.

IDENTIFICATION FORM

WRITE YOUR NAME:

Lee   Grace
LAST NAME   FIRST NAME

F Write. Say the word.

1. *F* or *f*   F IRST   ___irst   ___IRST
2. *L* or *l*   L AST   ___ast   ___AST
3. *N* or *n*   n ame   ___AME   ___ame

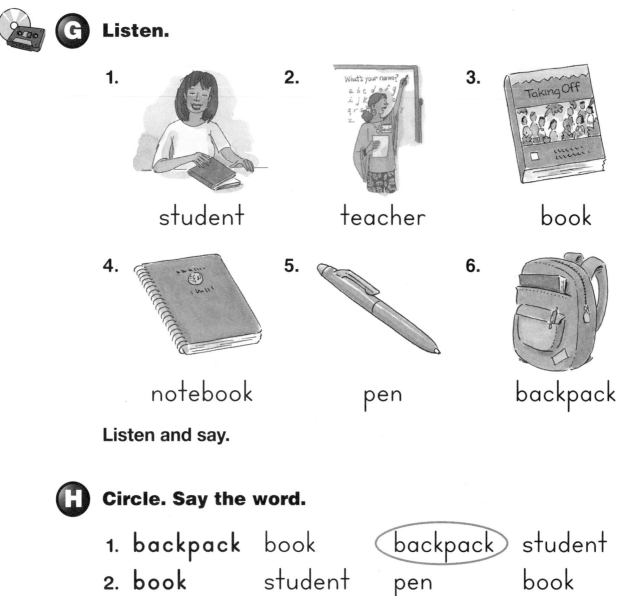

G Listen.

1. student

2. teacher

3. book

4. notebook

5. pen

6. backpack

Listen and say.

H Circle. Say the word.

1. backpack   book   (backpack)   student
2. book   student   pen   book
3. notebook   notebook   student   teacher
4. pen   backpack   notebook   pen

I **Write.**

1. 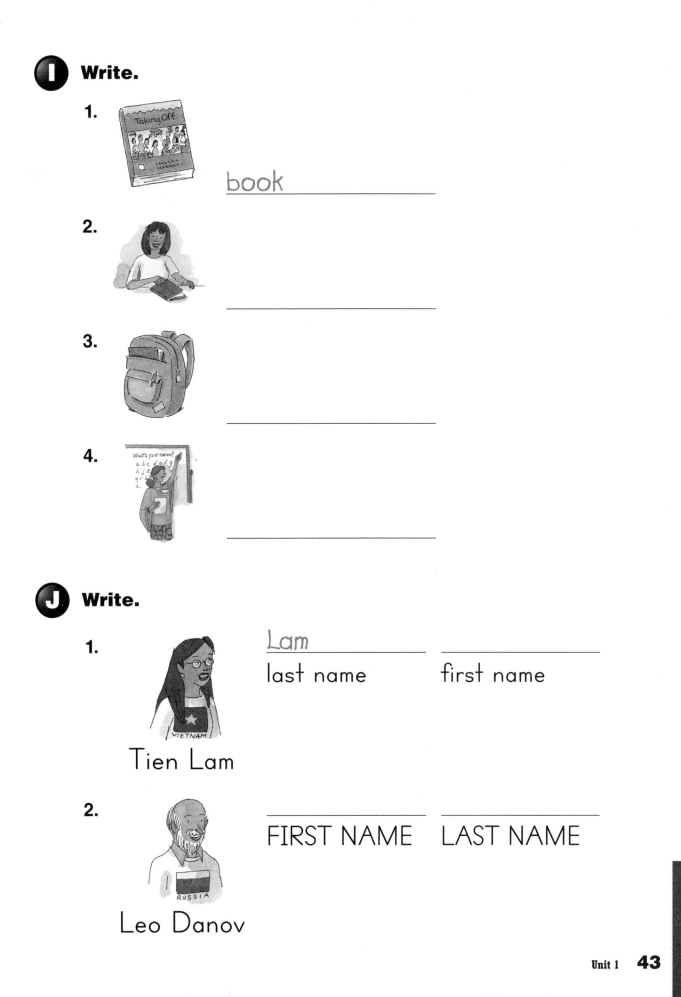 book _____

2. _____

3. _____

4. _____

J **Write.**

1. <u>Lam</u> _____
   last name   first name

   Tien Lam

2. _____ _____
   FIRST NAME   LAST NAME

   Leo Danov

A Listen.

C c   S s   Z z

Listen and say.

B Write.

1. Cc   _C_ ITY   _c_ ountry
2. Ss   ___ TREET   ___ ix
3. Zz   ___ ERO   ___ oo

C Circle.

1. COLOR   CODE   CLOSE   (COLOR)
2. STREET   STAY   STREET   STOP
3. zip   zip   sip   zap
4. zero   zone   nose   zero

D Listen and circle.

1. (state)　　street　　sixteen
2. city　　zip　　six
3. zip　　city　　dress

E Circle *CITY* and *City*.

1.
IDENTIFICATION FORM
TYPE OR PRINT

Los Angeles　　　California
(CITY)　　　　　　STATE

2.
Welcome to New York City

F Circle *STATE* and *State*.

1.
IDENTIFICATION FORM
PLEASE WRITE YOUR NAME, ADDRESS, CITY AND (STATE)

Leo V. Danov
NAME

1710 Sunset Street
ADDRESS

Los Angeles　　　CA
CITY　　　　　　STATE

2.
CALIFORNIA
000 000
The Golden State

G **Listen.**

1.

single

2.

married

3.

divorced

4.

widowed

Listen and say.

H ✓ **Check.**

	Single	Married	Divorced	Widowed
1.	✓			
2.				
3.				
4.				

Match.

address
city
name
state
zip code

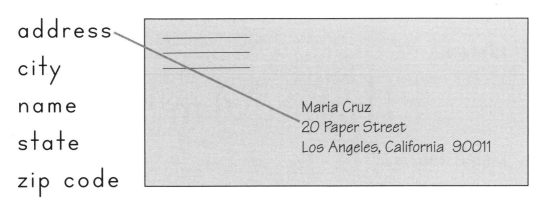

Maria Cruz
20 Paper Street
Los Angeles, California 90011

 Write.

| 10 Pen Street | Paul S. Lemat | Los Angeles |
| | 90015 | CA |

IDENTIFICATION FORM

TYPE OR PRINT

| Lemat | Paul | S. |
| LAST NAME | FIRST NAME | MI |

| | | | |
| ADDRESS | CITY | STATE | ZIP CODE |

A Listen.

Hh   Mm   Yy

Listen and say.

B Write.

1. Hh   <u>H</u> ER   <u>h</u> is
2. Mm   __ OTHER   fa __ ily
3. Yy   __ OUNG   prett __

C Circle.

1. HIS   (HIS)   HIT   HIM
2. MOTHER MISTER   MOTHER   MATTER
3. your   year   your   yes
4. husband husband   how   help

D Listen and circle.

1. you   (yes)   years
2. father   family   fine
3. mother   Maria   middle-aged

E Match.

_d_	1.	MOTHER	**a.**	father
____	2.	FAMILY	**b.**	daughter
____	3.	DAUGHTER	**c.**	family
____	4.	FATHER	d.	mother

F Read.

Children

Son

Father

Mother

Daughter

Family

G ✓ Check.

1.

___ father   ✓ family

2.

___ children   ___ son

H Circle.

1.   son   (daughter)

2.   father   son

3.   mother   father

4.   father   son

I Listen.

My name is Mary.
My mother's name is Yoko.
My father's name is Harry.
My brother's name is Mike.
This is my family.

Listen and say.

J Write. Say the sentence.

1. My name is <u>M</u>ary.
2. My mother's name is ___oko.
3. My father's name is ___arry.
4. My brother's name is ___ike.
5. T___is is ___y fa___il___.

K Write about you.

1. My mother's name is _____.
2. My father's name is _____.

A **Listen.**

Bb   Dd   Rr

Listen and say.

B **Write.**

1. Bb   <u>B</u> EDROOM   <u>b</u> ed
2. Dd   __ RESSER   __ esk
3. Rr   __ OOM   __ ug

C **Circle.**

1. BED   (BED)   BAD   DAB
2. DOOR   ROOM   DOOR   DO
3. read   red   dear   read
4. dresser   dress   dresser   dresses

D **Match.**

_c_	**1.** BED	**a.**	rug
____	**2.** DOOR	**b.**	tub
____	**3.** BEDROOM	~~**c.**~~	bed
____	**4.** RUG	**d.**	door
____	**5.** TUB	**e.**	bedroom

 E **Listen.**

1.
bathroom

2.
bed

3.
tub

4.
dining room

5.
dresser

6.
window

7.
rug

8.
refrigerator

9.
shower

Listen and say.

F ✓ **Check.**

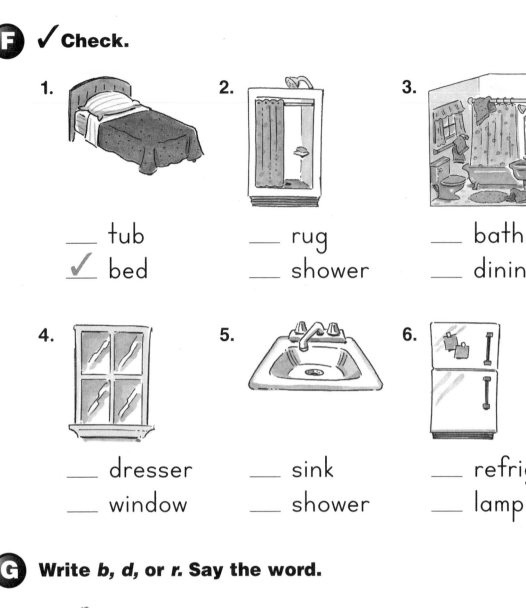

1.
___ tub
✓ bed

2.
___ rug
___ shower

3.
___ bathroom
___ dining room

4.
___ dresser
___ window

5.
___ sink
___ shower

6.
___ refrigerator
___ lamp

G **Write _b_, _d_, or _r_. Say the word.**

1. _r_ ug

2. ___ oor

3. ___ resser

4. ___ ath ___ oom

5. ___ ef ___ ige ___ ato ___

H **Listen and circle.**

1. bedroom   (bathroom)
2. dining room   living room
3. living room   bedroom
4. sink   tub
5. fireplace   closet

I ✓ **Check.**

	Kitchen	Living Room	Bedroom	Bathroom
1. bed			✓	
2. dresser				
3. refrigerator				
4. rug				
5. sofa				
6. tub				
7. window				

A **Listen.**

Aa   Ee   Tt

Listen and say.

 B **Write.**

1. Aa $\underline{A}$ PRIL   Mond $\underline{a}$ y
2. Ee   __NGLISH   r__ad
3. Tt   __UESDAY   __ime

C **Circle.**

1. APRIL   APPLE   (APRIL)   PAPER
2. EVERY   EVERY   EVER   NEVER
3. Thursday   Thursday   Thirsty   Tuesday
4. time   tame   time   mite

D **Match.**

<u>d</u> 1. SUNDAY   a. Friday

_____ 2. MONDAY   b. Monday

_____ 3. TUESDAY   c. Saturday

_____ 4. WEDNESDAY   d. Sunday

_____ 5. THURSDAY   e. Thursday

_____ 6. FRIDAY   f. Tuesday

_____ 7. SATURDAY   g. Wednesday

 E **Listen and circle.**

1. Sunday   Tuesday

2. Sunday   Monday

3. Saturday   Thursday

4. Monday   Friday

5. Saturday   Wednesday

6. Tuesday   Thursday

Match.

_f_   **1.** January

_____ **2.** February

_____ **3.** March

_____ **4.** April

_____ **5.** May

_____ **6.** June

a. Apr.

b. Jun.

c. Feb.

d. May

e. Mar.

~~**f.**~~ Jan.

G **Match.**

_b_   **1.** July

_____ **2.** August

_____ **3.** September

_____ **4.** October

_____ **5.** November

_____ **6.** December

a. Oct.

~~**b.**~~ Jul.

c. Aug.

d. Nov.

e. Sept.

f. Dec.

✓ **Check.**

		Day	Month
1.	August		✓
2.	Wednesday		
3.	Thursday		
4.	Oct.		
5.	July		
6.	Saturday		

I **Circle the month.**

1.
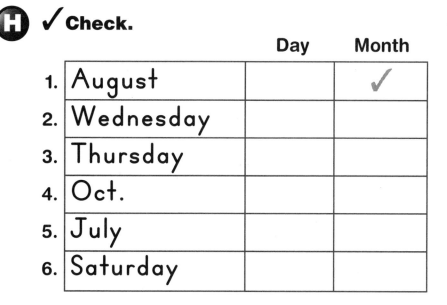

Identification Card

Name: Tien Lam

Date of Birth: (April) 4, 1980

2.

Tony's Video Store

Sandy Johnson

Expires: Nov. 1, 2010

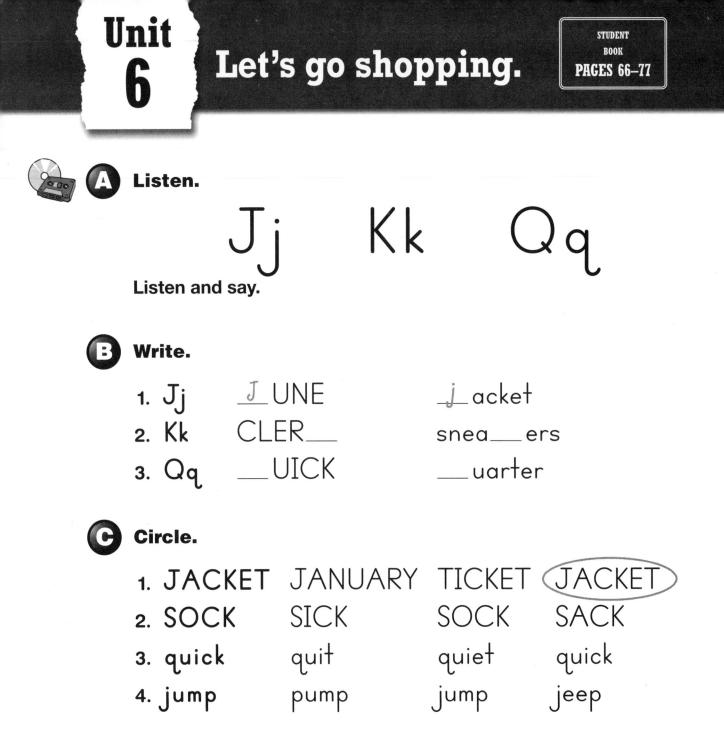

A Listen.

J j   K k   Q q

Listen and say.

B Write.

1. Jj   _J_ UNE   _j_ acket
2. Kk   CLER __   snea __ ers
3. Qq   __ UICK   __ uarter

C Circle.

1. JACKET   JANUARY   TICKET   ⟨JACKET⟩
2. SOCK   SICK   SOCK   SACK
3. quick   quit   quiet   quick
4. jump   pump   jump   jeep

 **D** **Listen.**

1.
dress

2.
sweater

3.
shoes

4.
suit

5.
shirt

6.
pants

7.
jacket

8.
watch

Listen and say.

E **Match.**

 C _____ 1. 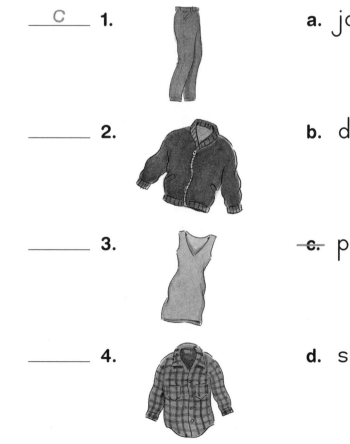   **a.** jacket

_____ 2.   **b.** dress

_____ 3.   ~~**c.** pants~~

_____ 4.   **d.** shirt

F Circle the word. Say the word.

1.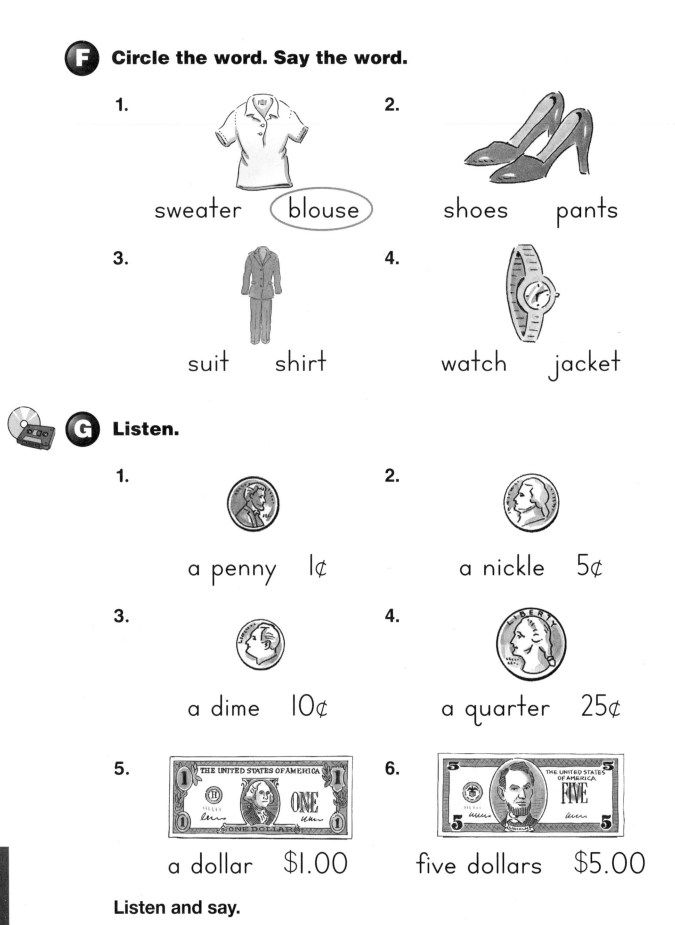

sweater   (blouse)

2. shoes   pants

3. suit   shirt

4. watch   jacket

G Listen.

1. a penny   1¢

2. a nickle   5¢

3. a dime   10¢

4. a quarter   25¢

5. a dollar $1.00

6. five dollars $5.00

Listen and say.

H **Circle.**

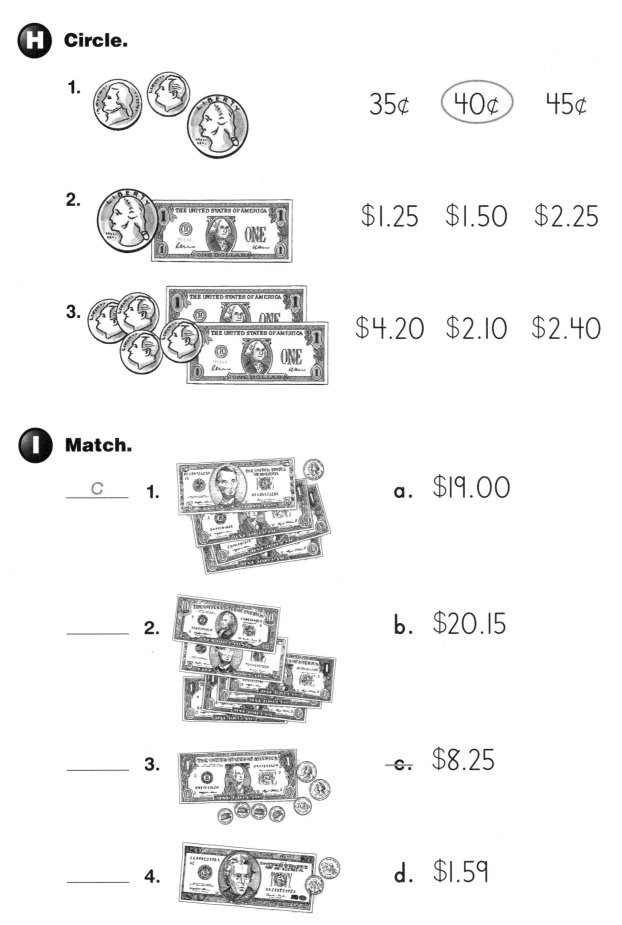

1. 35¢ (40¢) 45¢

2. $1.25 $1.50 $2.25

3. $4.20 $2.10 $2.40

I **Match.**

___C___ 1. **a.** $19.00

_____ 2. **b.** $20.15

_____ 3. ~~**c.**~~ $8.25

_____ 4. **d.** $1.59

I'm so hungry!

STUDENT BOOK PAGES 82–93

 A Listen.

Oo Uu Vv

Listen and say.

B Write.

1. Oo   _O_ NION   _o_ range
2. Uu   SO __ P   h __ ngry
3. Vv   __ EGETABLE   ha __ e

C Circle.

1. ORDER   OPEN   OVER   (ORDER)
2. BUTTER   BETTER   BUTTER   BATTER
3. have   have   heavy   hive
4. oil   old   oil   olive

D Write the letter. Say the word.

1. O or o   <u>O</u>RANGE   p__tat__es
2. U or u   j__ice   FR__IT
3. V or v   HA__E   __egetable

E Match.

<u> c </u>   1. butter   **a.** CARROTS

_____   2. carrots   **b.** ORANGES

_____   3. oranges   ~~**c.**~~ BUTTER

F Listen.

1. potatoes

2. apples

3. beef

4. chicken

5. butter

6. carrots

Listen and say.

G Write the number.

Shopping List
~~1. Bread~~
2. butter
3. chicken
4. eggs
5. fish
6. oranges
7. milk
8. potatoes

H Match.

_____d_____ 1.

a. bread

_____ 2.

b. cake

_____ 3.

c. ice cream

_____ 4.

~~d.~~ eggs

_____ 5.

e. milk

I **Listen and circle.**

1. (chicken)   lunch
2. cake   bread
3. juice   milk
4. apples   bananas

J **Read.**

Aisle 1	Aisle 2	Aisle 3
milk	carrots	chicken
butter	apples	beef
eggs	potatoes	fish

K **Circle the aisle from Activity J.**

1.    (Aisle 1)   Aisle 2   Aisle 3

2.    Aisle 1   Aisle 2   Aisle 3

3.   Aisle 1   Aisle 2   Aisle 3

4.   Aisle 1   Aisle 2   Aisle 3

Unit 8

How's the weather?

STUDENT BOOK
PAGES 94–105

A **Listen.**

Ii   Ww

Listen and say.

B **Write.**

1. Ii   __I__ T'S   l_i_ke   spr_i_ng
2. Ww   ___EATHER   ___indy   ___alk

C **Circle.**

1. I'M	IT'S	IN	(I'M)
2. WALK	WAIT	WALK	WORK
3. in	in	is	it
4. windy	winter	window	windy

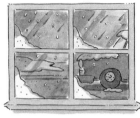 **D** **Listen.**

1. It's sunny.

2. It's snowy.

3. It's rainy.

4. It's windy.

Listen and say.

E **Match.**

___b___ **1.** **a.** It's windy.

_____ **2.** ~~b.~~ It's snowy.

_____ **3.** **c.** It's sunny.

_____ **4.** **d.** It's rainy.

F Read.

1.  walking

2. swimming

3. playing soccer

4. cooking

5. watching TV

6. reading

G Match.

_c_ 1.

_____ 2.

_____ 3.

_____ 4.

a. watching TV

b. playing soccer

c. swimming

d. reading

H Listen and write *i* or *w*.

1. T_i_en likes _w_alking and read__ng.

2. My name ___s Carlos. I like s__imming.

3. Grace l__kes play__ng soccer.

4. Leo likes ___atching TV. He likes ___alking, too.

 Look at Activity H. Complete.

1. Tien likes _____walking_____ and
   _____reading_____.

2. Carlos likes _____.

3. Grace likes _____ _____.

4. Leo likes _____ and
   _____.

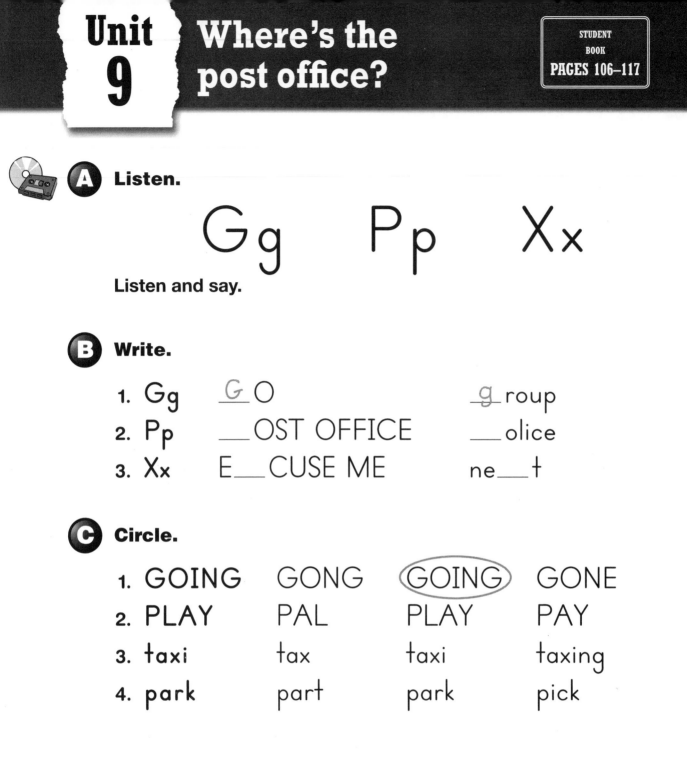

A Listen.

Gg   Pp   Xx

Listen and say.

B Write.

1. Gg   _G_ O   _g_ roup
2. Pp   ___OST OFFICE   ___olice
3. Xx   E___CUSE ME   ne___t

C Circle.

1. GOING   GONG   (GOING)   GONE
2. PLAY   PAL   PLAY   PAY
3. taxi   tax   taxi   taxing
4. park   part   park   pick

D Write the letter. Say the words.

1. G or g   _G_AS STATION   dru_g_store
2. P or p   hos__ital   SU__ERMARKET
3. X or x   E__CUSE ME   e__it

E Listen.

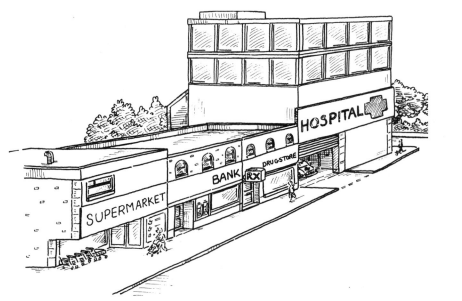

Listen and say.

1.

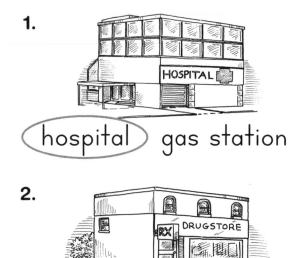

(hospital)   gas station

2.

bank   drugstore

3.

supermarket   gas station

4.

library   post office

5.

movie theater   bank

Section Two

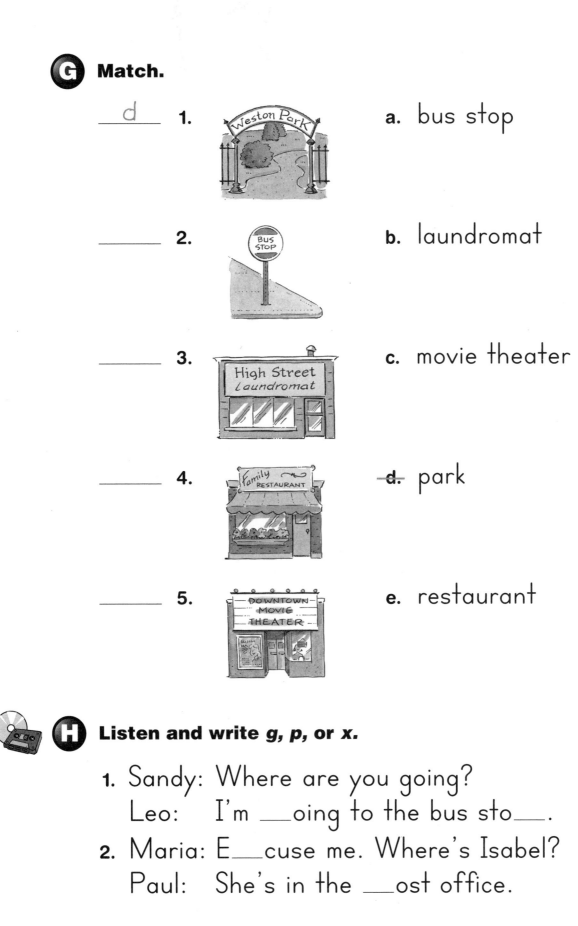

G **Match.**

<u>d</u> 1.

2.

3.

4.

5.

a. bus stop

b. laundromat

c. movie theater

d. park

e. restaurant

H **Listen and write g, p, or x.**

1. Sandy: Where are you going?
   Leo: I'm __oing to the bus sto__.

2. Maria: E__cuse me. Where's Isabel?
   Paul: She's in the __ost office.

A **Listen.**

1.

headache

2.

stomachache

3.

backache

4.

toothache

5.

cold

6.
sore throat

Listen and say.

B **Circle the word. Say the word.**

1.

(headache)   backache

2.

tootheache   cold

C **Read.**

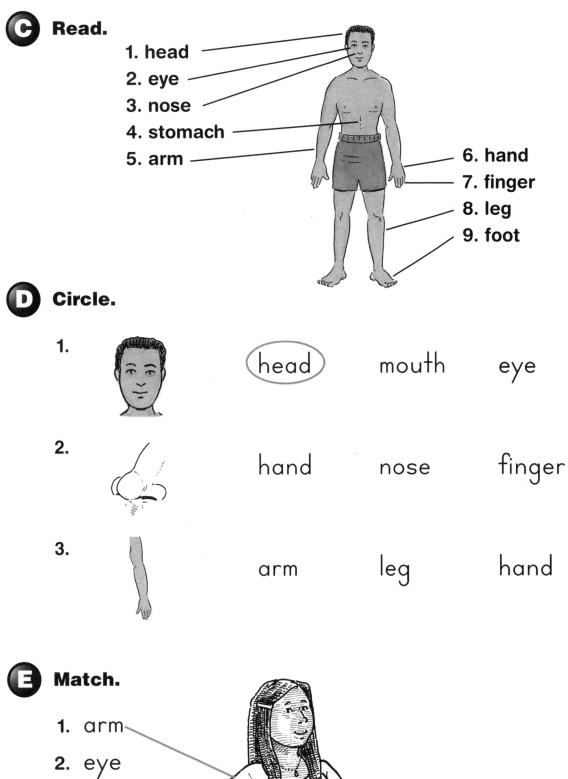

1. head
2. eye
3. nose
4. stomach
5. arm

6. hand
7. finger
8. leg
9. foot

D **Circle.**

1. (head)   mouth   eye

2. hand   nose   finger

3. arm   leg   hand

E **Match.**

1. arm
2. eye
3. finger
4. head
5. stomach

F **Write.**

1.  What's the matter with Don?
His ___hand___ hurts.

2. What's the matter with Leo?
His _____ hurts.

3. What's the matter with Ana?
Her _____ hurts.

G **Read.**

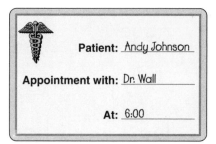

Patient: Andy Johnson

Appointment with: Dr. Wall

At: 6:00

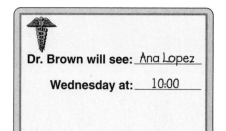

Dr. Brown will see: Ana Lopez

Wednesday at: 10:00

H ✓**Check.**

		True	False
1.	Andy has an appointment with Dr. Brown.		✓
2.	Ana has an appointment with Dr. Brown.		
3.	Andy's appoinment is at 6:00.		
4.	Ana's appointment is on Monday.		

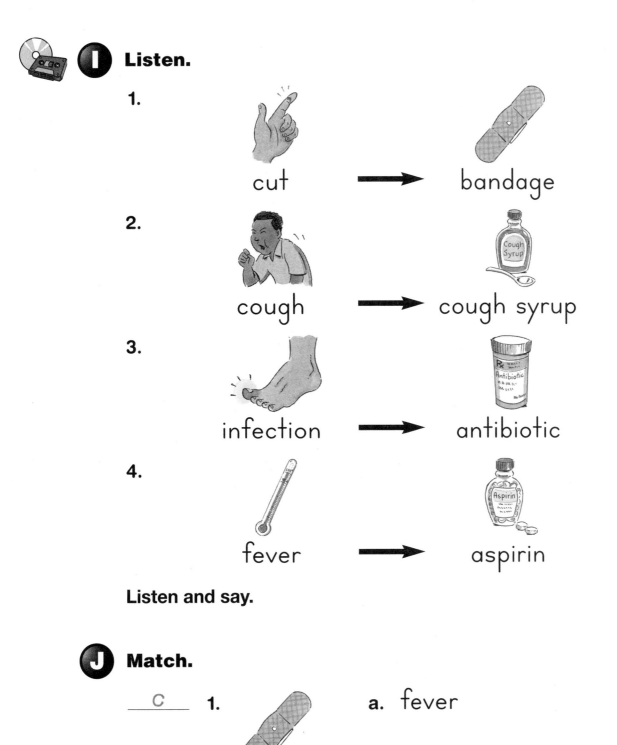

Listen.

1. cut ➡ bandage

2. cough ➡ cough syrup

3. infection ➡ antibiotic

4. fever ➡ aspirin

Listen and say.

J Match.

_C_ 1.   **a.** fever

____ 2.   **b.** cough

____ 3.   ~~**c.**~~ cut

A Listen.

1.

delivery person

2.

taxi driver

3.

gardener

4.
waiter

5.

cook

6.
cashier

7.
custodian

8.

receptionist

Listen and say.

B Write.

1.

_c_ _o_ _o_ _k_

2.

___ ___ ___ ___ ___ ___ ___

C Match.

<u>a</u> **1.** 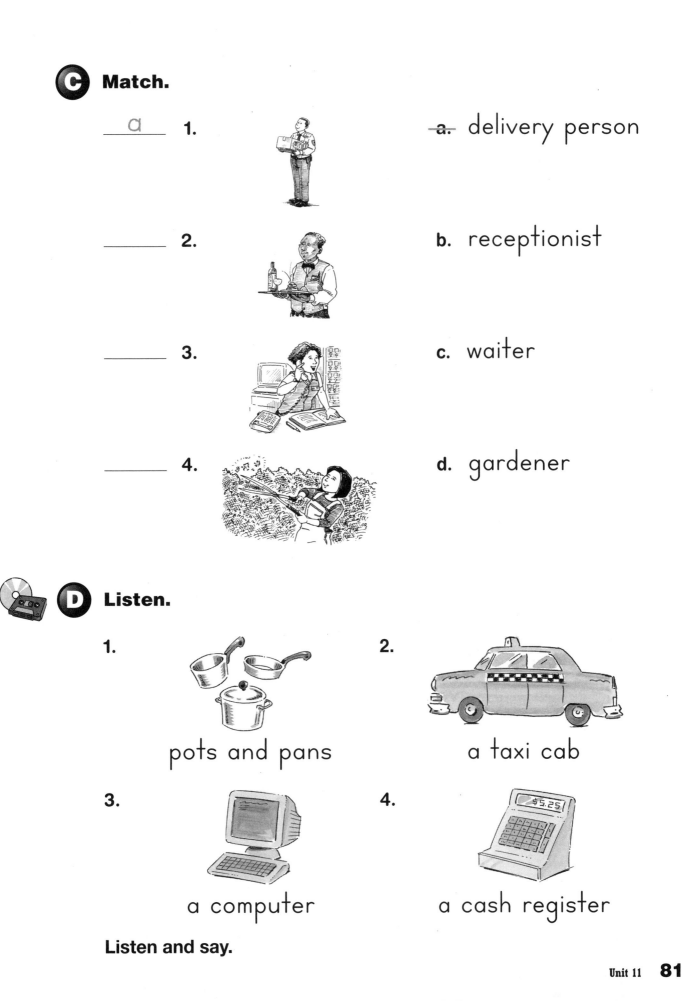   ~~a.~~ delivery person

_____ **2.**   **b.** receptionist

_____ **3.**   **c.** waiter

_____ **4.**   **d.** gardener

D Listen.

1. pots and pans

2. a taxi cab

3. a computer

4. a cash register

Listen and say.

Match.

<u>　b　</u> **1.** cashier

_____ **2.** cook

_____ **3.** taxi driver

_____ **4.** receptionist

a. computer

~~**b.**~~ cash register

c. taxi cab

d. pots and pans

 Read.

1.

drive

2.

use

3.

sell

4.

fix

G **Listen and circle.**

1. Leo can (drive a car.) use pots and pans.

2. Maria can   sell things.   use a cash register.

3. Paul can   fix things.   drive a car.

4. Grace can   sell things.   use tools.

H **Read.**

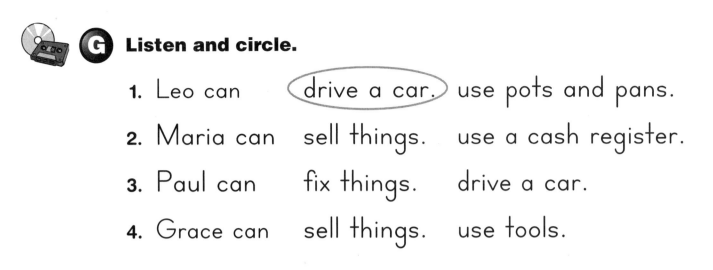

	MACEY'S		1379
		Date	2/22/05
Amount	SEVENTY-FOUR DOLLARS AND FIFTY CENTS		$74.50
PAY TO THE ORDER OF	Grace Lee		
		Carol O'Dell	

Grace Lee   1379

Pay Rate: $9.75/hour
Hours: 10
Gross Pay: $97.50

Deductions: $15.50

I **Read and ✓ check.**

		True	False
1.	This is Grace Lee's paycheck.	✓	
2.	Grace works at Macey's.		
3.	The check is for $50.97.		
4.	Grace makes $9.00 an hour.		
5.	Grace works 10 hours.		

A **Listen.**

1.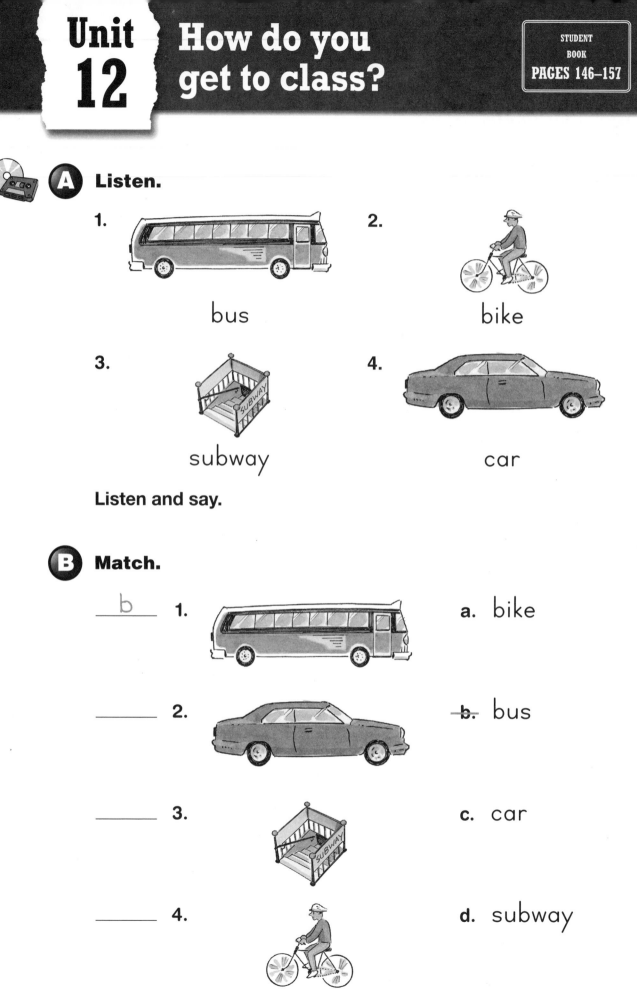

bus

2. bike

3. subway

4. car

Listen and say.

B **Match.**

_b_ 1. a. bike

___ 2. ~~b.~~ bus

___ 3. c. car

___ 4. d. subway

C **Listen and write.**

1. Leo drives his _____car_____ to school.

2. Will takes a _____ to work.

3. Paul rides a _____.

4. Don and Isabel take a _____.

D **Read.**

E **Write *left* or *right*.**

1. The supermarket is on the _____left_____.

2. The restaurant is on the _____.

3. The hospital is on the _____.

4. The post office is on the _____.

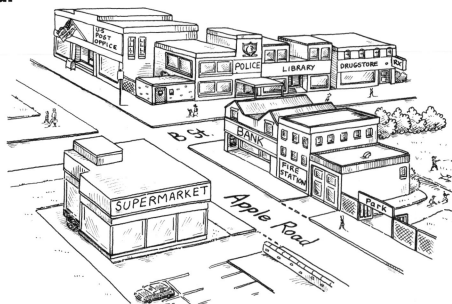

The supermarket is **on the corner of** Apple Road.

The bank is **across from** the supermarket.

The library is **between** the police station and the drugstore.

The park is **next to** the fire station.

G **Complete the sentences.**

1. The supermarket is ___across from___ the bank.

2. The police station is _____ the library.

3. The fire station is between the _____ and the _____.

4. The bank is _____ of B Street.

Read.

City	Leaves
Chicago	**10:15**
Miami	**11:30**
New York	**9:00**
Sacramento	**1:00**
Los Angeles	**10:45**
San Antonio	**9:30**
Washington, D.C.	**1:45**

I **Match.**

_b_ 1. Los Angeles   a. 9:00

____ 2. San Antonio   ~~b.~~ 9:30

____ 3. Sacramento   c. 10:15

____ 4. Washington, D.C.   d. 10:45

____ 5. New York   e. 11:30

____ 6. Chicago   f. 1:45

____ 7. Miami   g. 1:00

Listening script

Page 2
A. Listen.
T, I, L, H
Listen and say.

Page 3
A. Listen.
E, F, A, Y, X
Listen and say.

Page 4
A. Listen.
N, M, V, W, K
Listen and say.

Page 5
A. Listen and circle.
1. T
2. L
3. A
4. F
5. W
6. N
7. H
8. I
9. Y
10. M

Page 6
A. Listen.
U, C, O, Q
Listen and say.

Page 7
A. Listen.
P, R, B, D
Listen and say.

Page 8
A. Listen.
S, G, J, Z
Listen and say.

Page 9
A. Listen and circle.
1. Q
2. U
3. B
4. R
5. G
6. S
7. O
8. C
9. Z
10. B

Page 10
A. Listen.
l, t, i, j
Listen and say.

Page 11
A. Listen.
v, w, x, z
Listen and say.

Page 12
A. Listen.
o, c, a, e, s
Listen and say.

Page 13
A. Listen and circle.
1. t
2. i
3. w
4. m
5. a
6. o
7. c
8. e
9. x
10. z

Page 14
A. Listen.
u, r, n, h, m
Listen and say.

Page 15
A. Listen.
b, d, p, q
Listen and say.

Page 16
A. Listen.
y, g, f, k
Listen and say.

Page 17
A. Listen and circle.
1. u
2. k
3. d
4. h
5. f
6. j
7. b
8. y
9. p
10. g

Page 18
A. Listen.
A, B, C, D
Listen and say.

B. Listen and circle.
1. D
2. A
3. c
4. b

Page 19
A. Listen.
E, F, G, H
Listen and say.

B. Listen and circle.
1. G
2. E
3. h
4. f

Listening script

Page 20

A. Listen.
I, J, K, L
Listen and say.

B. Listen and circle.
1. J
2. K
3. i
4. l

Page 21

A. Listen.
M, N, O, P
Listen and say.

B. Listen and circle.
1. P
2. M
3. o
4. n

Page 22

A. Listen.
Q, R, S, T, U
Listen and say.

B. Listen and circle.
1. R
2. T
3. u
4. s

Page 23

A. Listen.
V, W, X, Y, Z
Listen and say.

B. Listen and circle.
1. V
2. Z
3. y
4. w

Page 30

A. Listen.
zero, one, two, three, four, five
Listen and say.

Page 31

A. Listen.
six, seven, eight, nine, ten
Listen and say.

Page 35

A. Listen.
A, B, C, D, E, F, G, H, I, J, K, L, M
Listen and say.

C. Listen.
a, b, c, d, e, f, g, h, i, j, k, l, m
Listen and say.

E. Listen and circle.
1. G
2. C
3. h
4. e

Page 36

A. Listen.
N, O, P, Q, R, S, T, U, V, W, X, Y, Z
Listen and say.

C. Listen.
n, o, p, q, r, s, t, u, v, w, x, y, z
Listen and say.

E. Listen and circle.
1. Z
2. O
3. s
4. u

Page 37

A. Listen.
0, 1, 2, 3, 4, 5, 6, 7, 8, 9, 10
Listen and say.

C. Listen and circle.
1. 4
2. 10

Page 40

A. Listen.
F, L, N
Listen and say.

Page 41

D. Listen and circle.
1. LAST
2. name
3. First

Page 42

G. Listen.
1. student
2. teacher
3. book
4. notebook
5. pen
6. backpack
Listen and say.

Page 44

A. Listen.
C, S, Z
Listen and say.

Page 45

D. Listen and circle.
1. state
2. zip
3. city

Page 46

G. Listen.
1. single
2. married
3. divorced
4. widowed
Listen and say.

Page 48

A. Listen.
H, M, Y
Listen and say.

Page 49

D. Listen and circle.
1. yes
2. family
3. mother

Listening script

Page 51

I. Listen
My name is Mary.
My mother's name is Yoko.
My father's name is Harry.
My brother's name is Mike.
This is my family.
Listen and say.

Page 52

A. Listen.
B, D, R
Listen and say.

Page 53

E. Listen.
1. bathroom
2. bed
3. tub
4. dining room
5. dresser
6. window
7. rug
8. refrigerator
9. shower
Listen and say.

Page 55

H. Listen and circle.
1. bathroom
2. dining room
3. bedroom
4. sink
5. fireplace

Page 56

A. Listen.
A, E, T
Listen and say.

Page 57

E. Listen and circle.
1. Tuesday
2. Monday
3. Saturday
4. Friday
5. Wednesday
6. Tuesday

Page 60

A. Listen.
J, K, Q
Listen and say.

Page 61

D. Listen.
1. dress
2. sweater
3. shoes
4. suit
5. shirt
6. pants
7. jacket
8. watch
Listen and say.

Page 62

G. Listen.
1. a penny, one cent
2. a nickel, five cents
3. a dime, ten cents
4. a quarter, twenty-five cents
5. a dollar
6. five dollars
Listen and say.

Page 64

A. Listen.
O, U, V
Listen and say.

Page 65

F. Listen.
1. potatoes
2. apples
3. beef
4. chicken
5. butter
6. carrots
Listen and say.

Page 67

I. Listen and circle.
1. chicken
2. bread
3. milk
4. apples

Page 68

A. Listen.
I, W
Listen and say.

Page 69

D. Listen and say.
1. It's sunny.
2. It's snowy.
3. It's rainy.
4. It's windy.
Listen and say.

Page 71

H. Listen and write *i* or *w*.
1. Tien likes walking and reading.
2. My name is Carlos. I like swimming.
3. Grace likes playing soccer.
4. Leo likes watching TV. He likes walking, too.

Page 72

A. Listen.
G, P, X
Listen and say.

Page 73

E. Listen.
Supermarket, bank, drugstore, hospital, post office, gas station, library
Listen and say.

Page 75

H. Listen and write *g, p,* or *x*.
1. Sandy: Where are you going?
   Leo: I'm going to the bus stop?
2. Maria: Excuse me. Where's Isabel?
   Paul: She's in the post office.

Page 76

A. Listen.
1. headache
2. stomachache
3. backache
4. toothache
5. cold
6. sore throat
Listen and say.

I. Listen.
1. cut, bandage
2. cough, cough syrup
3. infection, antibiotic
4. fever, aspirin
Listen and say.

A. Listen.
1. delivery person
2. taxi driver
3. gardener
4. waiter
5. cook
6. cashier
7. custodian
8. receptionist
Listen and say.

D. Listen.
1. pots and pans
2. a taxi cab
3. a computer
4. a cash register
Listen and say.

G. Listen and circle.
1. Leo can drive a car.
2. Maria can use a cash register.
3. Paul can fix things.
4. Grace can use tools.

A. Listen.
1. bus
2. bike
3. subway
4. car
Listen and say.

C. Listen and write.
1. Leo drives his car to school.
2. Will takes a bus to work.
3. Paul rides a bike.
4. Don and Isabel take a train.

G. Match.
1. b
2. c
3. e
4. a
5. d
6. f

Page 61

E. Match.
1. c
2. a
3. b
4. d

Page 62

F. Circle the word. Say the word.
1. blouse
2. shoes
3. suit
4. watch

Page 63

H. Circle.
1. 40¢
2. $1.25
3. $2.40

I. Match.
1. c
2. a
3. d
4. b

Page 65

E. Match.
1. c
2. a
3. b

Page 66

G. Write the number.

H. Match.
1. d
2. b
3. a
4. e
5. c

Page 67

I. Listen and circle.
1. chicken
2. bread
3. milk
4. apples

K. Circle the aisle.
1. Aisle 1
2. Aisle 3
3. Aisle 2
4. Aisle 2

Page 69

E. Match.
1. b
2. c
3. d
4. a

Page 70

G. Match.
1. c
2. a
3. d
4. b

Page 71

H. Listen and write *i* or *w*.
1. Tien likes walking and reading.
2. My name is Carlos. I like swimming.
3. Grace likes playing soccer.
4. Leo likes watching TV. He likes walking, too.

I. Look at Activity H. Complete.
1. Tien likes walking and reading.
2. Carlos likes swimming.
3. Grace likes playing soccer.
4. Leo likes watching and walking.

Page 73

D. Write the letter. Say the words.
1. GAS STATION   drugstore
2. hospital   SUPERMARKET
3. EXCUSE ME   exit

Page 74

F. Circle the words. Say the words.
1. hospital
2. drugstore
3. gas station
4. post office
5. bank

Page 75

G. Match.
1. d
2. a
3. b
4. e
5. c

H. Listen and write *g*, *p*, or *x*.
1. Sandy: Where are you going?
   Leo: I'm going to the bus stop?
2. Maria: Excuse me. Where's Isabel?
   Paul: She's in the post office.

Page 76

B. Circle the word. Say the word.
1. headache
2. cold

Page 77

D. Circle.
1. head
2. nost
3. arm

E. Match.
1. arm
2. eye
3. finger
4. head
5. stomach

Page 78

F. Write.
1. His hand hurts.
2. His finger hurts.
3. Her ear hurts. *or* Her head hurts.

H. Check.
1. False
2. True
3. True
4. False

Page 78

J. Match.
1. c
2. b
3. a

Page 80

B. Write.
1. cook
2. cashier

Page 81

C. Match.
1. a
2. c
3. b
4. d

Page 82

E. Match.
1. b
2. d
3. c
4. a

Page 83

G. Listen and circle.
1. Leo can drive a car.
2. Maria can use a cash register.
3. Paul can fix things.
4. Grace can use tools.

I. Read and check.
1. True
2. True
3. False
4. False
5. True

Page 84

B. Match.
1. b
2. c
3. d
4. a

Page 85

C. Listen and write.
1. Leo drives his car to school.
2. Will takes a bus to work.
3. Paul rides a bike.
4. Don and Isabel take a train.

E. Write *left* or *right*.
1. The supermarket is on the left.
2. The restaurant is on the right.
3. The hospital is on the right.
4. The post office is on the left.

Page 86

G. Complete the sentences.
1. The supermarket is across from the bank.
2. The police station is next to the library.
3. The fire station is between the bank and the park.
4. The bank is on the corner of B Street.

Page 87

I. Match.
1. TK
2. TK
3. TK
4. TK
5. TK
6. TK
7. TK

Writing practice

Writing practice